AF228473

HARRY KANE

BY TODD KORTEMEIER

WORLD'S **GREATEST** SOCCER PLAYERS

SportsZone

An Imprint of Abdo Publishing
abdobooks.com

abdobooks.com

Published by Abdo Publishing, a division of ABDO, PO Box 398166, Minneapolis, Minnesota 55439. Copyright © 2020 by Abdo Consulting Group, Inc. International copyrights reserved in all countries. No part of this book may be reproduced in any form without written permission from the publisher. SportsZone™ is a trademark and logo of Abdo Publishing.

Printed in China.
092019
012020

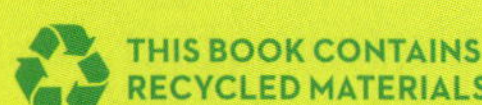

Cover Photo: Ina Fassbender/picture-alliance/dpa/AP Images
Interior Photos: David Klein/Cal Sport Media/AP Images, 4, 8, 28; Alastair Grant/AP Images, 7; Dominic Lipinski/PA Wire URN:42073983/Press Association/AP Images, 10; Nick Potts/PA Images/Getty Images, 13; Dan Istitene/Getty Images Sport/Getty Images, 15; Mike Hewitt/Getty Images Sport/Getty Images, 16; Julian Finney/Getty Images Sport/Getty Images, 18; Neal Simpson/EMPICS/PA Images/Getty Images, 21; Kirsty Wigglesworth/AP Images, 22; Tim Ireland/AP Images, 25; Antonio Calanni/AP Images, 27

Editor: Patrick Donnelly
Series Designer: Craig Hinton

Library of Congress Control Number: 2019942098

Publisher's Cataloging-in-Publication Data

Names: Kortemeier, Todd, author.
Title: Harry Kane / by Todd Kortemeier
Description: Minneapolis, Minnesota : Abdo Publishing, 2020 | Series: World's greatest soccer players | Includes online resources and index.
Identifiers: ISBN 9781532190629 (lib. bdg.) | ISBN 9781644943410 (pbk.) | ISBN 9781532176470 (ebook)
Subjects: LCSH: Soccer players--Biography--Juvenile literature. | Tottenham Hotspur Football Club--Juvenile literature. | European football--Biography--Juvenile literature. | Professional athletes--Biography--Juvenile literature.
Classification: DDC 796.3340922--dc23

TABLE OF CONTENTS

ONE OF
THEIR OWN

Harry Kane knew the importance of the North London Derby as well as anyone. He lived it as a boy. Kane grew up in North London as a Tottenham Hotspur fan, rooting desperately against Tottenham's archrival, Arsenal. Now he wore a Tottenham jersey as a player. Instead of watching his favorite club try to beat Arsenal in the English Premier League, Kane was doing it himself.

However, more than halfway through the match in February 2015, Tottenham trailed Arsenal 1–0. The home fans at White Hart Lane were hoping for some magic.

Harry Kane grew up dreaming about beating Arsenal in the North London Derby.

Tottenham delivered in the 56th minute. On a corner kick, Kane positioned himself at the far post. He watched as the ball soared in and the Arsenal goalkeeper batted it away. That's when Kane struck. He got to the loose ball first and fired it home to tie the game.

Kane was in the middle of a breakout season in 2014–15. The talented striker signed his first Tottenham contract in 2009. But it took him a while to break into the lineup. Once he got there, everyone could see what a special player he was. Kane and Tottenham had agreed on a new five-year contract earlier that week.

Scoring the tying goal in the North London Derby was special. But Kane had more work to do. The match was still tied in the 86th minute. Kane got into position in the attacking zone and waited for a pass. A teammate launched a long cross from well beyond the penalty area.

Kane celebrates after scoring the tying goal against Arsenal.

KANE
18

Kane outjumped an Arsenal defender and played the pass off his forehead. The ball ricocheted toward the net. The goalkeeper didn't have a chance. Tottenham's fans went into a frenzy over the game-winning goal.

Kane ran toward the crowd and slid feet-first. He pumped his fist and celebrated with the crowd. For Kane, the home fans really meant "home."

Kane got just enough on his header to send the ball into the Arsenal goal for the game-winner.

BORN TO SCORE
GOALS

Harry Kane was born on July 28, 1993, in Walthamstow, England. The hospital was located just 5 miles (8 km) from White Hart Lane, the stadium where he would one day play with Tottenham. He went to the same school that English soccer legend David Beckham had attended years earlier. It was no wonder he loved the sport.

Harry and his family were fans of Tottenham Hotspur, a team most fans refer to as Spurs. Like many Spurs fans, Harry's favorite player was forward Teddy Sheringham. Even early on, he admired players who could score goals.

Harry grew up near White Hart Lane, Tottenham's legendary stadium.

Harry was Tottenham blue through and through. But when Harry was eight, Arsenal invited Harry to join its youth academy. Harry played one season with Arsenal, Tottenham's biggest rival. But the Arsenal coaches thought he wasn't athletic enough and released him.

The release was devastating to Harry. But with the encouragement of his dad, he kept working. He played for his local club, the Ridgeway Rovers, and then he joined the academy at Watford, another club located nearby. During one game between Watford and Tottenham, the Spurs

Harry, *left*, fights for the ball while playing for Tottenham in the FA Youth Cup in January 2010.

coaches liked what they saw in Harry. They signed him to their academy at the age of 11.

Just as at Arsenal, Harry was not the fastest or the strongest player. But he had great natural ability. He shot the ball well. And he could play any forward position. He reminded the coaches a lot of Sheringham. In 2009, Harry committed to staying at the club and began playing with the Under-18 team.

In the 2009–10 season, Harry scored 18 goals while playing in 22 matches with Tottenham's U-18 squad. He even made the game-day roster for the senior team for two games. He never got off the bench, but even dressing for a Premier League team was an impressive accomplishment for a 17-year-old.

Harry signed his first professional contract in July 2010. But he had to wait a while to make an impact with Tottenham. Spurs decided to loan him to another local club, Leyton Orient, in January 2011. The move was designed for Harry to play senior-level matches, albeit

Before he could break into Tottenham's lineup full-time, Harry had to spend time on loan to Leyton Orient.

in a lower division. Harry wanted to play for Spurs in the Premier League right away. But the experience would prove valuable in developing his skills.

LOAN
LOWS

Playing for Leyton Orient in the third division, Kane made his first senior team start on January 22, 2011. In the 57th minute of the match against Sheffield Wednesday, he was left unguarded, and he deflected a free kick into the net. It was his first goal with a senior team. And it might have been the last time anyone forgot about Harry Kane.

Leyton Orient played in League One, two levels below Tottenham in the Premier League. And the club was at the bottom of League One when Kane arrived. His five goals in 18 games helped boost them to seventh place.

Tottenham gave Kane a trial on the senior team during Europa Cup action in 2011.

Kane had a successful run with Millwall.

Kane learned a lot of great lessons while out on loan. But there were times he wondered if he'd ever get a chance for Tottenham. In the fall of 2011, Kane played in six Europa Cup games for Spurs. He even scored his first goal in a 4–0 win in December.

But before Kane could make his Premier League debut, Spurs loaned him out again. This time he joined Millwall. The club was fighting to stay in the Championship, one level below the Premier League. If Millwall finished as one of the bottom three teams, it would be relegated down the English soccer ladder to League One.

Millwall fans are very passionate. Kane was only 18 and playing in a frenzied environment. But he handled it well. He scored seven goals in the final 14 matches of the season. Millwall was able to stay in the Championship. The fans loved Kane for the part he played. Kane liked playing for Millwall as well. But he still had eyes on breaking into the Spurs lineup.

Meanwhile, Kane got his first chances to represent his country in international play.

With England's U-19 team, Kane scored to beat France in the 2012 European championship. Kane scored six goals in 14 matches for England in 2012.

Kane hoped his play with Millwall and England would earn him a spot with Tottenham in 2012–13. Instead, the team loaned him out again, first to Norwich City and then to Leicester City. Worse, Kane didn't get much playing time for Leicester.

Kane considered quitting. But again, his dad inspired him not to give up. The next season, Tottenham wanted to send him on loan again. But Kane told the Spurs manager he didn't want to go. All he wanted was the chance to prove himself. He got it—and he didn't waste it.

Kane made his international debut for England's U-19 team in 2012.

BECOMING
A LEGEND

Kane has made a career of being in the right place at the right time. On April 7, 2014, he made his first Premier League start at home against Sunderland. In the 59th minute, a crossing pass came into the box. Kane darted for the ball and tapped it in. He spread his arms in celebration and took in the cheers of the home fans.

It was Kane's first Premier League goal. He scored only three that season, but bigger things were ahead. In 2014 Tottenham brought in a new manager, Mauricio Pochettino, who installed a new offensive system that

Kane celebrates his first Premier League goal on April 7, 2014, against Sunderland.

opened many scoring chances for Kane.

The 2014–15 season was Kane's breakout campaign. In October he netted his first hat trick. In December he scored in three matches in a row—all Tottenham wins. In January, he was named Premier League Player of the Month. He was rewarded with a new contract in February. Kane scored 31 goals in 2014–15 and was named the Premier League's Young Player of the Year.

With Kane's scoring role firmly established, Tottenham declined to bring back its other top forwards the next season. That put the pressure squarely on Kane, and he responded. Kane scored 25 goals to lead the Premier League. And he led Tottenham to third place in the league, its best finish since 1990.

Kane became a goal-scoring machine during his breakout season of 2014–15.

Before Kane arrived, Tottenham had been a relatively mediocre club—never terrible, but never truly great, either. But the club's status in the Premier League changed as Kane got settled in. Both the player and the club took another step forward in 2016–17. Kane led Tottenham to a second-place finish. And he led the league in goals again

with 29. Kane topped that with 30 goals in 2017–18, but he
lost out on his third Premier League scoring title.

In the middle of those two Premier League seasons,
Kane set a new league record. He scored 39 league goals
in 2017. That was an all-time record for a calendar year.
Kane was on his way to an amazing career. But he had one
task remaining.

England has a proud history in soccer. But the senior
men's team had become known for underachieving in
big tournaments. Kane was determined to change that.
In 2018, he was named England's captain for the World
Cup in Russia. And he quickly lived up to his billing.
Kane scored the first hat trick for England at a World Cup
since 1986. In total, he scored six goals in the tournament
to win the Golden Boot as England made a run to
the semifinals.

Kane celebrates one of his three goals against Panama during a
2018 World Cup match.

Kane continued his scoring ways during the 2018–19 season. Having emerged in recent years as a top Premier League team, Spurs were now regulars in the Champions League, a tournament for the best clubs in Europe. And in 2019 they made a magical run.

Kane scored four goals in the group stage. He added another in the round of 16. However, in the next match Kane injured his ankle. He was out of action for almost two months. His teammates carried on, though, driving the team to its first Champions League final. Fans were thrilled to see Kane return for the historic game. However, Spurs fell to fellow English team Liverpool 2–0.

It was a disappointing result. But with their hometown hero wearing Tottenham white, Spurs fans knew there was a chance they'd be back very soon.

GLOSSARY

box
Also called the penalty area, the marked area in front of the goal where a player is granted a penalty kick if he or she is fouled.

breakout
A performance or series of performances that signals a player is on the rise.

contract
An agreement to play for a certain team.

corner kick
A free kick from a corner of the field near the opponent's goal.

derby
An ongoing competition between two teams from the same region or city.

free kick
An unguarded kick awarded to a team after a foul.

hat trick
Three goals by the same player in one game.

loan
A club allowing a player to play for another team on a short-term basis.

manager
The head coach of a soccer team.

playmaker
The player who is responsible for a lot of his team's great plays.

relegated
Sent to a lower level of competition.

MORE INFORMATION

BOOKS

Avise, Jonathan. *Champions League Legends*. Minneapolis, MN: Abdo Publishing, 2019.

Marthaler, Jon. *Ultimate Soccer Road Trip*. Minneapolis, MN: Abdo Publishing, 2019.

Moussavi, Sam. *World Cup Heroes*. Minneapolis, MN: Abdo Publishing, 2019.

ONLINE RESOURCES

To learn more about Harry Kane, please visit **abdobooklinks.com** or scan this QR code. These links are routinely monitored and updated to provide the most current information available.

INDEX

ABOUT THE AUTHOR

A purple jersey, a gift from his father after a business trip to London, started a lifelong obsession with Tottenham Hotspur Football Club for Todd Kortemeier as a 12-year-old. On matchday you can find him in front of a TV somewhere in Minneapolis watching Spurs matches with his wife and dog.